I0500534

Gentle Recharging

52 Simple and Calming Meditation Exercises

A
Happiness Recharge
Book

Copyright © 2023 by Kelly Stone Cramer

All rights reserved. This book or any portion thereof may not be reproduced or used in any manner whatsoever without the written permission of the author except for the use of brief quotations in a book review.

ISBN - 13: 9798873046256

Content and artwork by Kelly Stone Cramer, founder of Happiness Recharge, LLC. www.HappinessRecharge.com.

The content of this book is not intended to be for medical use. The author disclaims any liability for actions taken by the readers.

It is advisable to avoid doing anything you do not feel safe doing or something incapable or dangerous for your body. You know your body best and know what it is comfortable and what should be avoided. Trust and listen to yourself.

Please visit a healthcare professional if you need help (asking for support is a sign of great strength). Take care of yourself always.

For dearly beloved L.R.D who, as Prince said it best, always celebrated "this thing called life."

Also dedicated to those searching for restoration and strength. Know that recharging to be your best self is easier to achieve when it is prioritized by you.

Preface

There is no wrong way to meditate. You could decorate a whole room with trinkets and art to get the right ambiance, or you could hide out on your bathroom floor for 10 minutes. Whatever way it works for you is the right way for YOU. Just be sure you're able to get into a comfortable enough position where you can feel relaxed, and hopefully not have any interruptions.

Before we get into the many benefits of meditation, let's touch on its foundation and essence. There is a lot to talk about here but for us to get right into the heart of the subject of discussion, we need to understand the genesis of meditation. Meditation originated in ancient India and its essence was to aid a deeper awareness of oneself.

Think about the basis of that. When was the last time you intentionally made time to know yourself at a deeper level? To be able to do such a thing, it would require you to slow down and tune into yourself – into your thoughts, into your reflections, into your hopes and dreams, and into your areas of growth. If you don't know where or how to get started, this is where this book will provide guidance.

The mind moves fast with thought. Combine that with our busy world, busy lives, family, friends, work, chores, errands, cooking, hobbies, exercise and so much more, slowing down can feel like an impossible and foreign task.

This book is written to make the process of going into meditation easy with short and direct exercises. It will reveal to you that meditation can be a powerful outlet that can allow you to tune into your own thoughts while tuning out the excess noise, distractions, and overstimulation of the world. It's a great way to peel off a layer of stress that can stand in the way of knowing yourself on a deeper level.

Other benefits one can experience through meditation are feelings of relaxation, recharging, a sense of peace, life balance, and even more happiness. The practice of meditation is a form of self-care, and it is a great investment in your well-being.

This book is a tool to help you be inspired to go within, reflect, and allow your inner voice to slow down and allow you a chance to be gentle with yourself. It can be your guide to let the quiet in and flow with a calmer sense of being.

These exercises are meant to help you find stillness in your life to decompress more and let go of heavy thoughts and stress. You can choose to either follow the sequence of this book in the order it is organized or you can flip randomly to a page to select the exercise that fits your purpose.

You can also practice these meditation exercises with a partner by each taking a turn to read the entries to one another so you can go deeper into focus with your own experience. Doing it solo works well too, by reading the exercise fully to understand the steps to take during your experience.

However you use this book, take pride in knowing you are taking this time for you to recharge. When you're recharged, you have the potential to have more energy to live a fuller life.

About the Author

Kelly Stone Cramer's credentials includes: a certified guided imagery meditation facilitator, motivational author, photographer, artist, retreat leader, and founder of Happiness Recharge LLC.

But more important than credentials, Kelly's mission is to help others feel strong and empowered to better themselves. This includes moving past stress, feeling calmer and healthier in the mind and body, and choosing self-care over people-pleasing.

Note from the Author

I created this book following a healing journey from three debilitating tickborne illnesses. For a while it was hard to trust that the healing was real, there to stay, and that my body was stable. Through my training as a certified guided imagery meditation facilitator, I created these exercises which allowed me to calm my mind, recharge and reconnect with my healthy body. Knowing they helped me was a validation that they could equally help others also in their recharging practices.

Whether you're new to meditation practices or are well versed in them, this book is an easy reference to use as it doesn't require hours of time each day.

Instructions before you begin each meditation

- Find a quiet place, if you can, where you will not be disturbed.
- Turn off or put your electronic gadgets in silence (phone, smartwatch, etc.). Light music is okay as you prefer.
- Wear comfortable clothing to your liking.
- Have a journal or notebook, and writing material - pen/pencil (electronic tool is okay too); when it feels right, you're encouraged to journal after a meditation even if the instructions don't include it in a specific entry. This reflection time is meant for you, and there is no wrong way or method to these practices.
- Have some water close to you as needed (closed cap if possible to avoid bumping into and having to clean up a spill, which can disrupt the flow of your exercise).
- Take a few deep breaths in and out to set yourself ready for the exercises.
- Take pride in the fact that you are making time for self-care, self-love, and personal recharging.

After your meditation exercise

- Slowly come back to your space. Blink your eyes open if they were closed; wiggle your toes and fingers to wake up the body; turn on some light music if you haven't already.
- Take a deep breath and exhale at your preferred pace.
- Do a few light stretches before you are fully upright or moving about.
- If you feel inclined, journal or take notes about your experience or how you are feeling.
- Drink some water. Hydrating after these exercises will help replenish your energy.
- Pat yourself on the back for taking this time to yourself to recharge and relax (really doing this may seem silly, but the action is a way of acknowledging that you've honored your well-being).

Meditations

Breathe

Preparation

Find a comfortable sitting position on the ground, a chair, or couch.

1

Meditation Exercise

For at least the next 10 minutes (more if you'd like), close your eyes, soften your facial muscles, and focus on your breath. It's okay to let your mind wander, but try to continue bringing your attention back to your breathing. When you're feeling relaxed, take a deep breath and let it out. Feel that your mind and body are relaxed into this exercise.

Purpose

Breath is an essential part of living. Focusing on your breath allows you to ground yourself and appreciate this foundational life source. Whenever you need to quiet your thoughts or take a break, this exercise is a good one to revisit. It allows you to get a better sense of how you are feeling while also calming your mind.

Note: It is okay if you doze off during this meditation. It may occur when you are relaxed and/or need rest.

Admire

Preparation

Sit in a sacred or favorite space of your choice. Grab writing materials or an electronic device for note-taking.

2

Meditation Exercise

Take a deep breath in and out to begin this exercise. Take in your surroundings with admiration and appreciation. Find one item to focus on and think about what it means to you. Perhaps, it represents something you are grateful for or maybe it reminds you of a happy experience. Think about how this item has helped you in some way; perhaps it helped you grow or grieve. Let your mind wander about this item and what it means to you.

Jot down some notes of gratitude and appreciation that come to mind in association with this object. You can sit with this as long as you'd like. You can also shift your attention to a new object if you'd like.

Purpose

Our surroundings should be supportive and reflect who we are and what we've experienced. Taking a moment out of the day to reflect on the items that surround you not only allows you to appreciate what is in your environment but it also allows you to reflect on yourself, your experiences, your life, and your thoughts in general.

Revisit this exercise any time you want to enjoy your environment and go deep in thought with what your surroundings mean to you.

Dance

Preparation

Make sure you have on some comfortable clothing you can move in. Next, put on some of your favorite music that you feel relaxed, motivated, or inspired by. Clear a space around you so you have a bit of room to move around – enough, at least, to extend your arms fully.

3

Meditation Exercise

Start by standing in the center of your space. Take a deep breath in and out. Listen to the music you have chosen to play. Pay attention to how it makes you feel.

Let this feeling out by beginning to move your body with the music. Let your limbs, hips, head, or whatever else you find wants to move, sway, bop, or spin with the beats and sounds. There are no wrong movements here. Dance, move, listen, and feel as long as you'd like.

Purpose

This exercise is meant to allow you to move with the inspiration you feel. It allows your mind and body to connect with the sounds you hear and the movement you make. It adds a whole new meaning and importance to dancing around your room.

Stretch

Preparation

Wear comfortable unrestrictive clothing that allows you to move freely. Find an open space where you can easily move your arms and legs.

4

Meditation Exercise

Start by standing with your arms at your sides. Take a few deep breaths in and out. Identify in your body where you may feel tension and add movement to that area. If it's your shoulders, roll your shoulders forward and backward as many times as it feels comfortable. When you're ready, begin to stretch your limbs one at a time and pause for at least 10 seconds with each stretch. Do not push yourself to the point of pain. Continue taking deep breaths in and out throughout each stretch.

You can stretch in any motion that feels comfortable to you. For your legs, it could be sitting on the floor with your legs straight out while you reach your arms toward your feet. It could be standing while your legs are straight and you let gravity help you stretch your lower body, while your upper body hangs down with arms loosely hanging to the floor. For your arms, you could use one to hold the other across your chest in a straightened position. You could also bend one arm at a time and reach over your shoulder, aiming for your palm to touch your back while the other palm holds your elbow in place.

Continue with these stretches in as many positions as you'd like and for as long as you'd like. Revisit this exercise often to keep your body loose and flexible.

Purpose

This exercise is meant to help you release tension in your body through motion and stretching. It also allows you to relax while increasing flexibility. It not only allows for a better mind-body connection, but it's also a mindfulness exercise that allows you to focus on your intentional movement and breathing.

Listen

Preparation

Get in a comfortable sitting or lying down position. Place in some headphones and play some of your favorite relaxing music.

5

Meditation Exercise

Close your eyes and take a deep breath in, then slowly let it out. Sink into the sounds you are hearing. Feel the sounds, beats, and lyrics (if there are any) within your whole body as if the acoustics are bouncing around your insides.

Continue to take deep breaths in and let them out slowly.
Allow your body to relax; feel rejuvenated and restored with this music.

Purpose

This exercise is meant to relax and calm you at a deep level through the power of music.

Hear

Preparation

Get in a comfortable sitting position.

6

Meditation Exercise

Take a slow deep breath and let it out. Notice if you're holding any tension in your body, like your face or shoulders, and relax those areas. Close your eyes. Pay attention to what you hear. Listen to the sounds in your immediate surroundings, off in the distance, and even the sounds coming from you, like your breath.

At this moment, you are an observer of the sound. Next, pay attention to how these sounds make you feel. There is no wrong way to feel, just tune into the sensations. Sit with these sounds and sensations as long as you'd like. Open your eyes when you feel completion with this exercise.

Purpose

The purpose of this exercise is to raise your awareness by being an observer of your environment and to yourself through sound. It is also meant to allow you to acknowledge your feelings and emotions through focus and observation.

Observe

Preparation

Bring a notebook or electronic device for note-taking. Go to a public place where there are other people around.

Find a place to sit comfortably.

7

Meditation Exercise

Take a deep breath in and let it out. Relax any area of tension you may hold in your body. Then, take a look around your environment. Observe the things you notice.

Notice how you feel in this setting. Acknowledge what elements around you make you feel - ease or discomfort. Now observe others around you. Look for body language or expressions from others. Notice the feelings that come from you while you're observing. Do you feel comfortable or uncomfortable with what is occurring around you?

Use your notebook or electronic device to take notes of your observations of your surroundings and the observations of your own sensations. When you feel you have gathered enough to reflect on, pack up your items and go home or to a place you will be alone or uninterrupted.

When you're in a private space, review your notes. Reflect on one observation at a time. Think about why it stuck out to you as an observation and think about why it may have made you feel the way it did. Go through all your observations and emotions till you have reflected upon them all.

Purpose

The purpose of this exercise is to get in touch with how you're feeling with your own emotions, to slow down and be more present, and observe what and who is around you and how they make you feel. It is also intended as a demonstration that the more you tune in to yourself, the more you can trust your own thoughts, feelings, and instincts.

Reflect

Preparation

Grab a notebook or electronic device to use for note-taking. Get in a comfortable sitting position.

8

Meditation Exercise

Close your eyes and take a deep breath in, then let it out. Think about one main thing that has been heavy on your mind as of late. Reflect on why this may be causing you discomfort or worry. Next, picture this situation turning in your favor and working out perfectly and positively. Envision yourself happy and shining with joy. Take a deep breath in and let it out.

Next, take out a notebook or electronic device and jot down the issue that made you feel stressed. Then, jot down what you envisioned with things working out in your favor. Make note of how you felt and what you were doing to celebrate this victory.

Revisit this visualization any time you are feeling tense about any situation that weighs on your thoughts.

Purpose

This exercise is meant to ease worry and practice positive thinking. This is also an intentional reflection to identify the source of stress, and shift it into something lighter. Transmuting worry into uplifting feelings can change your outlook and mindset.

Touch

Preparation

Find a favorite item you possess and either sit next to it or hold it in your hands. Have a notebook or electronic device near you to jot down notes.

9

Meditation Exercise

Sit comfortably in a place where you won't be easily distracted or disturbed. Touch your item with your hands and fingertips. Let the texture seep into your senses. Notice if it is soft or smooth or hard or slick. Take in how this feels in your hands and against your skin.

Reflect on what this item means to you. Does it stir up a memory or an ambition? Does it bring you comfort in any way? Take down some notes to reflect on how you feel and why.

Purpose

The purpose of this exercise is to tap into your sense of touch and associate it with your emotions. Making this connection more often allows you to experience life at a deeper sensory level.

Relax

Preparation

Get in a comfortable lying down position in a quiet place where you won't be distracted or disturbed.

10

Meditation Exercise

Start by taking a deep breath, then let it out. Next, tighten, flex, and hold all your muscles – everywhere from your face, your arms, clench your fists, tighten your legs, down to your toes. Hold everything tightly for at least 10 seconds. Then, release it all at once and relax everything.

Take a deep breath and sink into where you lay as you feel the release in your facial muscles, your arms, hands, legs, and feet. Feel that every part of your body is relaxed.

Lay in this relaxed position for as long as you'd like. Focus on your breath. Notice if tension has gone back to any place in the body and release it again.

Purpose

The purpose of this exercise is to let go of any tension in the body. By flexing all the muscles at once, when it's released, the mind can't focus on the parts that typically hold tension. Do this exercise when you're feeling tension in your body to shift to a state of relaxation.

Energize

Preparation

Have writing materials or an electronic device handy.

11

Meditation Exercise

Sit in a comfortable position. Close your eyes and reflect on what uplifts you, makes you feel happy, and brings a smile to your face. This could be an activity or a person or a mental state.

When you have a few things in mind, open your eyes and make a note of these things in a list. Review your list, and of these items, make a note of the one item you couldn't live without. Know that this is what energizes you the most at this time. Understand that it is important to prioritize this the most.

Purpose

The purpose of this exercise is to identify what generally energizes you and what energizes you the most. Know that the result of what energizes changes over time, so revisit this exercise as often as you need.

Appreciate

Preparation

Have writing materials or an electronic device handy.

12

Meditation Exercise

Get in a comfortable sitting position. Close your eyes and picture someone you admire and appreciate in your life. Notice how they make you feel and what it is about them you appreciate.

Next, jot down a note about who this person is and what you admire and appreciate about them. Do this a couple more times, or as many times as you wish.

As a bonus, now that you know the who and the why, tell these people sometime how you feel. It will uplift them and make you feel good too.

Purpose

This exercise allows you to have a deeper understanding of who you are drawn to in your life and what kind of values they hold, which are a reflection of your own values. This also allows you to be more connected to your heart with your connections with others because appreciation comes from love.

Value

Preparation

Have writing materials or an electronic device handy.

13

Meditation Exercise

Get in a comfortable sitting position. Close your eyes and picture something you feel gratitude toward. This could be anything from meeting a basic need to ways you have been allowed to grow in your life. It could involve people or tools, or emotions. Let yourself feel how valuable this is to your senses and what it has meant to you in your life.

When you're ready, open your eyes and make note of what it is you value, what it is you feel grateful for, and how it has changed your life for the better. Repeat this exercise until you have at least a few items on your list. Keep this list handy (available for daily viewing) as a reminder to yourself of your values and gratitude.

Purpose

This exercise allows you to see what you cherish and appreciate the most in your life. Having it as a common reference allows you to feel grateful regardless of what you are going through.

Rekindle

Preparation

Get in a comfortable sitting position.

14

Meditation Exercise

Close your eyes and take a deep breath in, then let it out. Next, place your hands on a place on your body where you have felt shame or frustration and picture the color pink around your hands while you send love to this part of your body.

Take some deep breaths in and out when you do this. Continue moving to other parts of your body till you have given love to each area you haven't always appreciated.

Purpose

This exercise allows you to rekindle self-love for areas of your body that have been underappreciated, be that from external beliefs or physical pain or any other personal reason.

Smell

Preparation

Grab at least three things (can be more) readily available to you that have a pleasant smell to you (i.e., soap, candle, spices, lotion, perfume, flower, shampoo, etc.). Get in a comfortable sitting position and place these items in front of you.

15

Meditation Exercise

Selecting one item, pick it up, close your eyes and breathe deeply to take in its smell. Let the scent relax you and let your mind wander.

Maybe it brings in a memory or a feeling of relaxation. Continue doing this with one item at a time and allow yourself to enjoy these scents that bring you a personal experience.

Purpose

This exercise is meant to stimulate relaxation through your sense of smell. This is also a popular practice called aromatherapy where you can find a lot of scented oils to add to your practice. Starting with the things that are around also works well and can have a stronger association with your life as you are around these smells more often.

Recollect

Preparation

Find a picture (framed or digital) of yours that is tied to a happy memory. Get in a comfortable sitting position and set the picture in front of you.

16

Meditation Exercise

Take a deep breath in, then let it out slowly. Now hold the picture in your hands and take it in. Think of what this image means to you and take notice of how it makes you feel. Who or what in this image evokes happy emotions and why. Ponder these answers and recollect any other feelings this brings up for you.

Next, set the image aside, close your eyes and take a deep breath in and let it out. Now, picture yourself in the scene of that image you were just holding. Notice your surroundings and how you are feeling at this moment. Allow yourself to be immersed in this image as if it is happening right now. Sit with this and be in this setting as long as you'd like.

When you're ready to step out of the scene, take a deep breath in and let it out. Then, slowly blink your eyes open.

Purpose

This exercise is meant to get you closer to a happy moment or feeling by getting closer to an image you enjoy. It may even allow you to relive some happy feelings you experienced in the past, which can make those feelings alive in the here and now.

Preparation

Wear comfortable loose-fitted clothing. Get in a place spacious enough where you can move around to at least extend your arms to full length.

17

Meditation Exercise

For the next 10 minutes, move your body in slow-motion activities. You can do normal activities or flow with some repetitive movements, but slowly.

Notice where your patience is and if your mind slows. Focus on both your movements and your breath. Know there is no wrong way to move here (just be sure to be gentle and not cause yourself pain in the movements).

This exercise is inspired by Tai Chi, the art of gentle movements and breathing, and also a practice of defense training; movements of Tai Chi were originally inspired by birds.

Purpose

This experience is meant to not just slow the body, but also slow and calm the mind.

Still

Preparation

Get in a comfortable sitting or lying down position.

18

Meditation Exercise

Close your eyes. Let your muscles relax. Besides breathing, hold still in this position for at least 10 minutes; you can go for longer if you like.

Your mind can wander any way it wants. Just focus on your stillness.

Purpose

This exercise allows you to appreciate stillness in your body and mind. By doing this practice often, you may find that you enjoy the stillness and feel more centered. It may allow you to notice when you're moving too fast in your life, which goes outside your natural rhythm.

Hum

Preparation

Find a comfortable place to sit or lie down.

Disclaimer: This one may trigger your comfort level. If so, take notice as it's also a good exercise to use your own sound. Making noise can seem like an intrusion around others, but you deserve to make noise. You deserve to make ripples. You deserve to exist.

19

Meditation Exercise

Close your eyes and take at least five to 10 minutes to hum in between breaths. It can be any tone (low, high, or anywhere in between) you'd like or even a variation of tone.

Pay attention to how you're feeling during this exercise. Notice the vibration through your body from the sound you're creating. Let your mind wander to become clear during this time. There is no wrong way. The more you do this though, the more likely it is for your mind to become clear where you're just focusing on the hum.

Purpose

The purpose of this exercise is to both allow yourself to make noise as a symbol of existence and also allows you to relax and feel the simple yet powerfully calming tones, which come from you, within your mind and body.

Stand

Preparation

Find a solid wall to lean against in whatever standing position that makes you most comfortable.

20

Meditation Exercise

Close your eyes and take a deep breath in, then let it out. Next, visualize tree roots flowing from your feet into the ground. See them going deep into the earth, grabbing hold of a solid foundation. Notice how this makes you feel strong and sturdy in your body. You also notice how connected you feel to the earth and all life. Take a few deep breaths in and out slowly. Stay here as long as you'd like.

When you're ready, visualize the roots pulling back upward, back to your feet, until you are no longer connected to the earth. Feel your feet's mobility once more and come back to the sense of standing against a wall.

Purpose

This exercise is meant to make you feel strong in your body while also feeling connected to your environment. Revisit this exercise often when you need to feel grounded and balanced.

Roll

Preparation

Find a space you can move around in, enough to span out your arms.
Wear comfortable clothing.

21

Meditation Exercise

Begin in a standing position and raise your arms out straight to make a t-shape. Next, make small circle motions with your arms for 20 seconds or however long feels comfortable. Shift the circular motion to your wrists.

Then, place your arms on your hips and roll your waist and hips in a slow circular motion, like you're hula hooping. Next, brace your hand against something to lift your leg up a few inches off the floor and move your full leg in a circular motion. Then, shift that down to your ankle and rotate it slowly. Move to the other leg and ankle as well.

Move any other part of your body in a circular motion you'd like. Once you're done, shake out your limbs and feel the warmth and easier movement of your body.

Purpose

The purpose of this exercise is to allow your body to feel more limber, loose, and warm through gentle and slow movements. It doesn't take much to get things flowing and it can make a lot of difference in the ease of movement throughout your day.

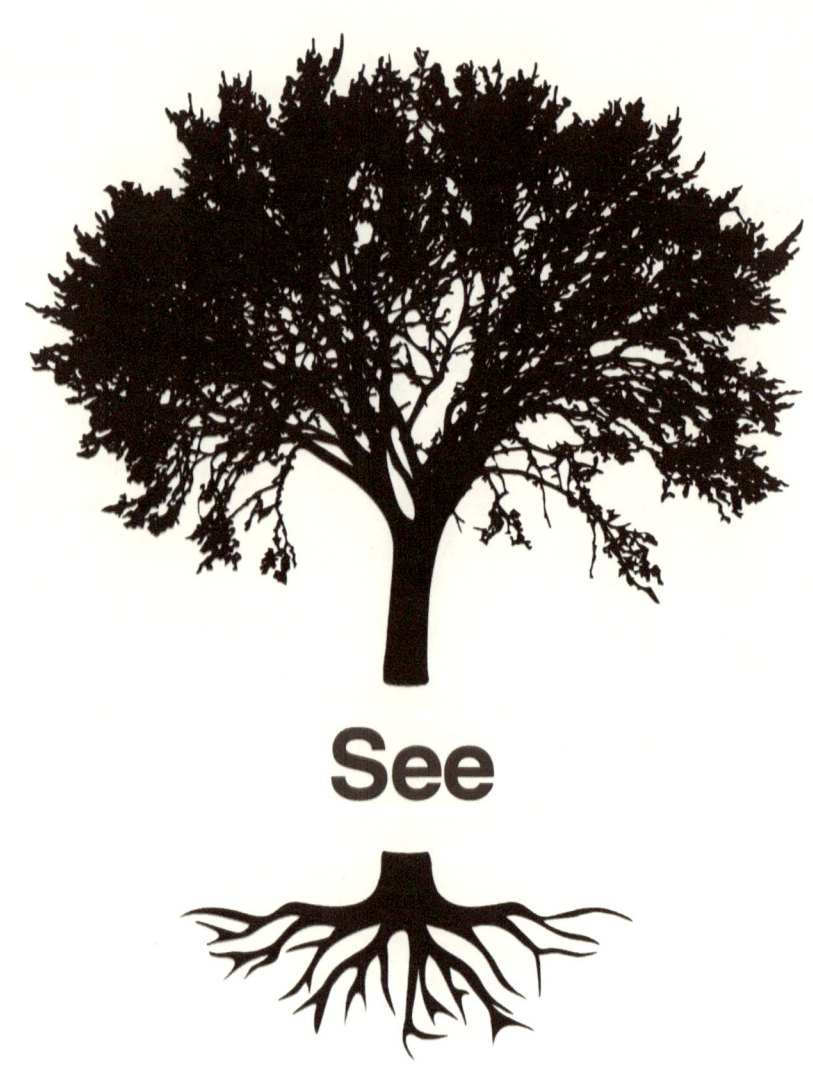

Preparation

Get in a comfortable sitting position.

22

Meditation Exercise

Take a deep breath in, then let it out. Observe your surroundings and select one color to notice in the space you're in. For example, if it's red, notice all the spots of red in your space that stand out to you. Once you have noticed everything in one color, shift to another and observe everything of that color in your surroundings.

Repeat this for as many colors as you'd like. With each color, notice if any of these colors stood out to you and why. Did it make you feel a certain way because of its vibrancy, or perhaps it was because of a specific object?

Purpose

This exercise allows you to be more in touch with your surroundings and in tune with your emotions beyond just passively looking at things.

This exercise allows you to slow down enough to really see your surroundings by paying closer attention to their details, starting out by breaking them down with something as simple as color.

Hydrate

Preparation

Get yourself a glass of water. Feel free to dress it up with ice or lemon if you'd like.

23

Meditation Exercise

Take your time to drink this whole glass of water. With each gulp, feel it easily gravitating down your esophagus to your stomach. Understand that this essential liquid allows you to be hydrated but also is the reason you are able to live.

While water is a simple and available substance, allow yourself to feel appreciation for it within your body. Recognize the importance of hydrating often to help your body do its best.

Purpose

The purpose of this exercise is to take a pause and hydrate your body while appreciating the life-giving benefits of water. Simple water gives so much to us. If you can appreciate something as basic yet profound as water, what else in your life can you find deep appreciation for?

Feel

Preparation

Get in a comfortable sitting or lying down position.

24

Meditation Exercise

Once you're ready, take a few slow deep breaths. Then pinpoint how you are feeling at this moment. Ask yourself why/what the source of this feeling may be from. Ask yourself why again and again until, like the core of an onion, you reach the inner layer. Then sit with this feeling. Allow yourself to feel whatever it is you're feeling.

Note if any action is now needing to be taken after this exercise, such as self-care.

Purpose

This exercise is meant to peel back the layers of reason to reveal the source of an emotion. The ability to do this for yourself is powerful, as it allows you to have a deeper understanding of your feelings. Take pride in this exercise as it can be challenging to go deep. The more you do this activity, the easier you can apply it to truly knowing yourself.

Fly

Preparation

Get in a standing position.

25

Meditation Exercise

With your eyes open, take a deep breath in and out. Continue breathing deeply at your own pace. Place your arms to your sides and when you take a deep breath in, extend your arms straight out to your sides, parallel with your shoulders, and then reach them up to the sky and extend them above your head. As you exhale, place them down to your sides again.

Continue to do this for at least five to 10 minutes at the pace you're comfortable with.

Purpose

This exercise allows you to relax while filling your space in a graceful movement.

Revisit

Preparation

Get in a comfortable sitting or lying down position.

26

Meditation Exercise

For the next 10 to 15 minutes, close your eyes and visualize one of your favorite places. This could be a favorite memory or a place where you feel at peace. Notice how you feel and sink into this vision by taking deep breaths at your own pace.

Purpose

This exercise is intended to make you feel grateful for the vision and joyful for how it makes you feel.

Walk

Preparation

Put on comfortable clothes and layers for the outdoors along with appropriate walking shoes or footwear.

27

Meditation Exercise

While walking is not typically something you may think of as a meditation activity, this is going to be a mindfulness exercise.

Go outside on a walk, where you feel safe and comfortable, for at least fifteen minutes. During this walk, be very mindful of your actions - the sounds of your footsteps, your breath increase as you walk, and how your legs and arms move based on your terrain. Pay attention too to what you see. Take it all in and notice how it makes you feel.

Purpose

This exercise is meant to build your awareness and also allows you to be more mindful of living in the moment.

Calm

Preparation

Get in a comfortable sitting position.

28

Meditation Exercise

Close your eyes and relax your face. Take a deep breath in, then pucker your lips tight so that when you exhale, air passes through slowly. Do this a few times and then breathe normally.

When you're ready, do this again. You can do this as many times as you wish.

Purpose

This exercise is meant to slow you down and calm your mind and body. By concentrating on your slow breath out, you can feel your body relax.

Scan

Preparation

Get in a comfortable lying down position.

29

Meditation Exercise

Picture a large glowing hoop hovering above your head. This hoop is going to be your placement indicator of where you are putting your attention.

Picture the hoop slowly moving down your body toward your feet. As it passes each part of your body, notice where you are holding tension and relax those muscles. You can picture the hoop going as slow or as fast as you want, and you can do as many scans as you need to feel relaxed.

Purpose

This exercise is meant to relax all the parts of your body. This visualization also helps you to focus on something specific so you can have a deeper relaxation experience.

Uncoil

Preparation

Start in an uncomfortable position. Maybe cross your arms and your legs or place your hands behind your body, crossing each other. Don't push yourself to the point of pain, just a position that isn't your normal state.

30

Meditation Exercise

Slowly begin to move one arm or leg at a time and place yourself in a more comfortable position. It's important to just have one move at a time.

After each move, take a deep breath in and let it out. Keep positioning yourself until you have found the most comfortable position possible. Even if you think you've reached it, you can keep making moves between breaths to test out new positions.

Purpose

This exercise is meant for you to move with purpose and be in tune with how your body feels. It is also a demonstration that you can always make more moves for your benefit.

Simulate

Preparation

For this exercise, you'll want to use a smartphone or computer for research purposes. Have writing materials handy.

31

Meditation Exercise

Open Google or another search engine and type the word: relaxation. Then, click "images" below the search bar.

Next, scroll through all the images at your own pace. Notice if you are feeling relaxed or entering a more calm state. Keep scrolling for at least five minutes or more. Take deep breaths throughout this simulation exercise.

Notice which images you were drawn to most or which allowed you a sensation of peace. Take your writing materials or electronic device and jot down some notes, phrases, or words about what images triggered your relaxation response. You may even want to note some of the activities you want to do in the near future and action steps about how you will make them happen.

Purpose

This exercise is meant for you to observe something visual and feel what you are seeing.

Seek

Preparation

Get in a comfortable sitting or lying down position. Have writing materials handy.

32

Meditation Exercise

Close your eyes and take a deep breath in and out. Visualize something you wish to achieve. If nothing initially comes to mind, let your thoughts wander to picture yourself a couple of years from now to find some ideas. Once you have something in mind, picture it having happened. Picture yourself in the moment of it happening. Notice how you're feeling in that moment, what you're doing, who or what surrounds you. Picture what you're wearing, if you're holding anything, if you're sitting, standing, and so forth. Picture yourself as this achiever of what you seek today and take a mental snapshot image that sticks out in your mind that you can picture anytime at a later date.

After your visualization, open your eyes and grab a notebook, journal, or electronic device. Jot down some notes on what you envisioned, how you felt, and any further details you can recall. Be sure to describe the mental snapshot you took in your mind. Lastly, in your notes, create three columns and add a header at the top of each to show: weekly, monthly, and annually. Then under each header, list a few action items for yourself to get you closer to this achievement.

Purpose

This exercise is to show yourself, from a relaxed state, what it is you want and seek. In addition, it can show you that you have the power to create actions to get you closer to reaching what it is you seek.

Focus

Preparation

Get in a comfortable sitting or lying down position.

33

Meditation Exercise

Close your eyes and take a few deep breaths in and out. Then, continue to breathe normally. Put all your focus on your breath. Pay attention to the rise and fall of your body as the air goes in and out. Take deep breaths as you would like. Spend at least 15 minutes focusing on your breath and observing it as you become more relaxed.

Purpose

This exercise is meant to pull your attention to one thing so it calms your mind and relaxes your body.

Notice

Preparation

Get in a comfortable sitting or lying down position.

34

Meditation Exercise

Close your eyes and sit as still as possible for a moment. In this stillness, notice where you may be holding any tension. Notice where you may be compensating in your position for any weakened parts of your body. Notice if you're feeling any pain in your body.

Then, reposition your body in a new way and do the exercise again. Notice where you may be holding tension, where you're compensating, or where there is pain.

When you feel you're holding tension, let your muscles relax. When you feel compensation, adjust to a more comfortable position. Where you feel pain, place your hands over that spot and send love and gratitude to your body that allows you to move throughout your day.

Continue this exercise till you have done at least four to five different positions.

Purpose

This exercise is meant to raise your awareness of how you are feeling physically. It is also meant to release tension and find appreciation for your body.

Float

Preparation

Get in a comfortable sitting or lying down position.

35

Meditation Exercise

Close your eyes and take a few deep breaths. Let what has been heavy on your mind or causing stress enter your awareness like a thunderstorm.

Visualize your stress in the storm clouds so much that you can only see the cloud itself.

Now, see that clouds and the storm begin to lesson, float away, and dissolve into a blue sky.

Now, take a few deep breaths and focus your attention on your breath.

Purpose

This exercise is meant to put your mind at ease and give you a reprieve from the stress in life.

Count

Preparation

Get in a comfortable sitting or lying down position.

36

Meditation Exercise

Close your eyes and take a few deep breaths in and out. When you're relaxed. Take a deep breath in and as you take a breath out count how many seconds it takes you to breathe out. Take another deep breath in and at your next deep breath out, add a second to that breath.

Continue adding seconds to your breath out till you've reached a limit (don't push yourself here). Once you've reached your maximum amount of seconds you're comfortable spending while breathing out, do this a few more times and then breathe normally.

Purpose

This exercise is meant to calm your mind and your body deeply with intentional and focused breathwork.

Retrospect

Preparation

Get in a comfortable sitting or lying down position.

37

Meditation Exercise

Close your eyes. Take a few deep breaths in and out. Picture yourself standing in front of a mirror. Instead of seeing your current reflection, you see your child self. Everything you do, they reflect back.

Be with your child reflection for a while. Admire them. Send them love by giving yourself a self-hug, a big smile, and even blow a kiss. When you feel you're ready, say goodbye with a big wave as you see them do the same.

Purpose

This exercise is a method of self-love by way of your inner child and your current self.

Uplift

Preparation

Get in a comfortable sitting or lying down position. Have writing materials handy.

38

Meditation Exercise

Close your eyes. Picture yourself on your best day. This can be a day that has happened already or a day you hope to live. Picture yourself beaming with happiness.

Notice how you feel, what you are doing, what you are wearing, and who or what is around you. Keep picturing this while taking deep breaths in and out as you want. Notice when you're taking the breaths and what you're picturing.

When you're ready, open your eyes and jot some things down in a notebook or electronic device. Write down what you pictured. If it was a day you were hoping for, write about what kinds of goals that may have come from this. If it was a day that has already happened, write about what brought you the most joy.

Purpose

This exercise is meant to uplift you by envisioning your happiest self.

Love

Preparation

Get in a comfortable sitting position.

39

Meditation Exercise

Close your eyes and take a few deep breaths, then let them out slowly. Picture another you sitting in front of you. They are positioned the same, look the same, and are exactly the same. Lean forward a bit and hold out your arms to embrace yourself with a loving hug. Feel yourself relax and also be supported in this self-hug.

Purpose

This exercise is to demonstrate that a source of strength and love can come directly from you.

Release

Preparation

Get out a candle and light it. Stand or sit behind it at a table.

40

Meditation Exercise

Think of something that has been weighing on you. This can be something that has been causing you stress or something you've been carrying around, like a trauma. Close your eyes and still be thinking of what ails you.

Next, place your hands at your sides and then as you take a breath in, place your palms up toward the sky and raise them from your hips to your chest. At your exhale, rotate your hands outward, facing the wall, form them like a ball and breathe out. Continue doing this motion, breathing in with your arms and hands going from your sides to your chest, while pushing out your breath in a ball to the wall. You can do this as fast and forceful or as slow and gentle as whatever comes out.

When you're done, open your eyes and say out loud, "I release you," as many times as you'd like. You're encouraged to add more words here about what it is you specifically release. They could be one-word items like fear, anger, pain, etc. Then, once you are done with your release words, blow out your candle. Next, say some things you'd like to welcome into your life, such as, "I welcome in love; I welcome in strength; I welcome in health." You can say as many things as you'd like to welcome in. When you're done, take a few deep breaths. Be gentle with yourself following this exercise.

Purpose

This exercise is meant to help you release and let go of what weighs you down while welcoming in good things you'd like to add or increase in your life. It is a powerful tool so you can carry on with strength and heart.

Flow

Preparation

Get in a comfortable sitting or lying down position.

41

Meditation Exercise

Start by closing your eyes and taking a deep breath in, then let it out. Let yourself just be in this comfortable position and hold space for anything that comes into your mind. Let it rattle or slowly move around your thoughts.

When you're ready to let that thought go, focus on taking a deep breath in and let it out. Take another deep breath and let it out. All the while, your attention is on the breath going in and out of your body.

Next, again, hold space for anything that comes into your mind. Sit with that thought or thoughts for a bit and start the breathing cycle again with all your focus and attention on your breath. Continue with this flow until you feel relaxed and lighter from the thoughts that came and went.

Purpose

This exercise is meant for you to flow gently with whatever thoughts come to you while also switching focus on your breath to find release and relaxation.

Relate

Preparation

For this exercise, you will need to be around nature. You can either sit near or amongst nature (i.e., inside: at a window or near a houseplant or vase of flowers; outside: on a blanket or bench or on a nature walk). However you incorporate nature will be right for you. Have writing materials handy.

42

Meditation Exercise

Observe the nature you have selected. Take it in with admiration. Notice its parts. Pay attention to what comes to mind when you're observing. Perhaps you notice its resilience for growth, its beauty, its strength. Sit and observe as long as you'd like. You can do some slow deep breathing here with your eyes closed or open, or you can just sit with appreciation.

Next, take out a notebook or electronic device to write with and jot down all the things you observed (list form or paragraph form is fine). Next, read over your writing and recognize that your observations are not your opinions, but they also live inside you too. Nature is nature regardless of the words you use to describe it. These words come from you and are a part of you. What you recognize in your environment, you can relate to within yourself. Lastly, jot down where you identify in yourself the things you observed and why.

Note some things you may be striving to become and don't sell yourself short of the things you already are; these correlations can help prove this to yourself.

Purpose

This exercise helps you to connect with nature by finding things you relate to. It is also a method of showing yourself that you are amazing and strong, just like the beautiful nature you admire.

Acknowledge

Preparation

Start by grabbing a notebook or an electronic device to take notes. Get into a comfortable sitting position.

43

Meditation Exercise

Make a list of 10 things you feel grateful for in your life. This could be re-lated to your relationships, health, experiences, lessons, environment, or any specific thing that you hold dear to your heart.

Once you have a list, select one of your favorite items. Next, close your eyes and visualize this thing you are grateful for. Acknowledge why you are grateful for this thing and allow yourself to feel all the positive feelings connected to this. Take deep breaths in and out as you feel these good feelings.

Next, select another item on this list and do the same visualization about why you're grateful and feel all the positive feelings associated with what you have chosen. Make sure you are taking deep breaths along the way. Continue with this exercise until you have visualized all the 10 items you listed. Once you're done, make a note in your notebook or device about how you feel at this moment.

Purpose

This exercise is meant to make you identify and acknowledge what you are grateful for in your life. It is also a method of appreciating and feeling uplifted for the goodness that is part of your life.

Amplify

Preparation

Get in a comfortable sitting or lying down position.

44

Meditation Exercise

Close your eyes. Take a few slow cleansing breaths in and out. Picture your whole body glowing with bright radiant, white and gold light. This light is so bright that sparks are flickering all around you. Now imagine this glowing light expanding larger around your body like a ring. As you're imagining this ring, think about all the things you hope for in your life. As you picture them, imagine they are being absorbed into this light. Keep picturing your hopes, wishes, ambitions, and anything you aim for in your life.

Once you have thought about all you can, picture the ring of light growing further and further beyond yourself. Picture it going past your room, past the space or building you're in, past the city you're in, past the land, past the sky, past the atmosphere, picture it growing into space around the earth and once it reaches space, picture it flashing out fast beyond the stars and into the abyss. And as fast as it flashed beyond into space, you see it coming back fast in a flash. It comes back from the depth of space, back to the atmosphere, back to the sky, back to the land, back to your city, back to where you are, back to the space you're in, and back to you. Picture the glowing light surrounding you as it did at the beginning. See the flickers begin to simmer slowly and absorb back into your body along with the glow. Take a few slow deep breaths in, then exhale out. When you're ready, open your eyes.

Purpose

This exercise exemplifies, expanding out the exuberant light that lives within you (and all your passionate ambitions) into the universe and back. It is a powerful symbolic practice to put your intentions out into existence and own it from within.

Honor

Preparation

Have a journal or electronic device near you so you can use it during this exercise if needed. Get in a comfortable lying down position.

45

Meditation Exercise

Close your eyes. Take a few deep breaths. Next, place your hand over the center of your chest and notice how you are feeling. Take note of this stillness if there is something your body or mind needs at that moment or in the near future. If the need is immediate and it is a basic need, you are encouraged to pause and address it right away. If it is a need in the near future, you can pause and make a note so this doesn't slip your mind.

Next, proceed by continuing to take a few deep breaths, still with your hand placed in the center of your chest. Picture your hand begin to emanate a glowing light that alternates between white and pink. Be still with this radiant light of yours and know it is you honoring yourself with love, support, and strength. Be with this as long as you'd like. When you're ready to transition back into your day, picture this light softening to a dull glow and then your body absorbing it into your center. Notice how you feel and journal about it if that feels right.

Purpose

This exercise is a way of honoring yourself by addressing your immediate needs and showing yourself love and support. Know that it is something you can repeat any time you are in need of an uplifting self-boost.

Soothe

Preparation

Have a journal or electronic device near you to take notes following this exercise. Find a comfortable position sitting or lying down.

46

Meditation Exercise

Close your eyes. Take a few deep breaths in and out. Think of a spot on your body that has been giving you discomfort or pain. This could be happening now or recently. Next, place your hand(s) over this spot as a symbol of support, comfort, love, and recognition. Let your hands rest there for as long as you'd like. Notice your touch and warmth, while acknowledging that this part of your body, although causing discomfort, is still working hard and doing its best.

Reflect on whether there is anything in your power that you can do to alleviate any discomfort or pain in this area (be that stretching, exercise, rest, or something else that comes to mind).

When you're ready, open your eyes and take your journal or electronic device and jot down some notes for a self-reference. Note the place on your body you were focusing on and if there is anything you can do in your power to lessen any pain or discomfort.

Purpose

This exercise is meant to provide support for yourself while living in the understanding that even though a part of you may not be perfect, it's striving to serve you as much as possible. Recognizing this is an act of self-love and self-acceptance.

Alchemize

Preparation

Have a journal or electronic device near you. Get in a comfortable position sitting or lying down.

47

Meditation Exercise

Take a few deep breaths in and out. Close your eyes. Start by thinking of one or two emotions that you have felt uncomfortable with lately (i.e., anger, sadness, etc.). Next picture this emotion (one at a time if you have multiple of them) as a child.

Observe this child and this emotion. Understand that this is how you've been feeling. Envision yourself going over to comfort the child. Notice how your comfort supports and soothes them. The emotion in the child shifts to joy and you see happiness on their face. They reach out to you and give you a hug. In this moment, their joy becomes a part of you.

Take a few deep breaths and open your eyes. Take some time to journal about this experience.

Purpose

This exercise is meant to allow you to separate yourself from difficult emotions while giving yourself comfort and support.

Free

Preparation

Get in a comfortable position sitting or lying down.

48

Meditation Exercise

Start by taking a few deep breaths in, then let them out. Close your eyes. Start by envisioning a field of dried dandelions dancing slightly in the wind.

Next, envision what has been causing you distress in your life in the field of dried dandelions – resting among the dried seeds. You notice the wind picking up and as they do, the seeds, along with your stress begin to pull away from the dandelion heads.

One after the other they are pulled out by the wind until they have all been plucked and are gone in the distant breeze.

Take a deep breath in, then let it out. Revisit this visual exercise any time you need to let stress go out of your life.

Purpose

The purpose of this exercise is to envision something relaxing and easy, then pair it with something that is harder to picture and more challenging to let go. By combining something simple with something complex, it is easier to release. This tool can be applied to any stress you want to dissipate in your life.

Move

Preparation

You can play light music for this exercise if you wish. Be sure you are wearing some comfortable clothing in a space you can move in.

49

Meditation Exercise

Stand in a comfortable position with your arms at your sides. Stand up straight and take a deep breath in, then let it out. Next, say a goal out loud that you have for yourself. After you've spoken your goal, lift your arms out to form a "T" shape. Next, motion both arms in circle motions. They can be big circles or small circles, whatever you feel comfortable doing. Switch from forward circles to backward circles. Do these arm circles as long as it feels comfortable. Take deep breaths while you are in motion. When your arms are tired, listen to your body and let them rest at your sides.

Next, move your legs from side to side. Start with your legs in place and side step one leg to the side as wide as you're comfortable doing, and let the other leg follow. Alternate leg side stepping to keep the motion balanced. You can add motion by swaying your arms if that feels comfortable. There is no wrong way to do this movement, it's what feels natural and comfortable. When you're done moving, say your personal goal out loud once more. Notice if you've said this goal differently or if you feel any different vs. the first time you said it.

Purpose

This exercise is meant to allow comfortable movement in your body while also noticing that goals can become stronger after allowing motion through your body.

Preparation

Get in a comfortable sitting or lying down position. Have writing material or an electronic device near you.

50

Meditation Exercise

There is no wrong way to be. Whatever it is you are doing or feeling is you. Perhaps you feel deep, so breathe deeply. Perhaps, you are stressed, so let it out with movements. Perhaps, you are reaching for improvement, so stretch out your body. Perhaps, you want to improve your relationships, so care for them like you would a growing plant. Perhaps, you want to deepen your peace, so sit calmly and let your mind chatter and eventually slow.

Therefore, in this moment now, once you're done reading this exercise, sit in a comfortable position, close your eyes and just breathe. Let yourself be. Let yourself be in whatever that looks like or feels like. Breathe. Observe. Breathe. Be.

When you're ready, take some notes about how you feel and your favorite ways to be you.

Purpose

This exercise is meant to allow you to recognize that you are perfect in this moment. Regardless of your expectations or goals, how you are right now is glorious. Even if you are having a difficult time, recognize you are showing up for yourself and striving for improvement. What is more glorious than that?

Soften

Preparation

Play some gentle music if you'd like. Sit or lay in a comfortable position.

51

Meditation Exercise

Close your eyes. Take a deep breath in, then out. Relax your body by noticing if you are holding any tightness in your muscles - jaw, shoulders, brow, or any other place you typically flex.

Take a few deep breaths. Feel your body relax deeper into your position. Let your mind wander to wherever it needs. When you want to clear your thoughts, focus on taking a deep breath in and out. Feel your body and mind relax into a sense of calm. Continue to be in this position and breathe as long as you'd like. Allow yourself to soften and find a state of gentle recharging.

Purpose

This exercise is meant to relax your mind and body in a soft and gentle way. Revisit this often for an easy way to find your natural state of calm.

Live

Preparation

Find a comfortable place to sit or lie down. Have a journal or electronic device nearby in case you'd like to take notes during or after this exercise.

52

Meditation Exercise

A lot of miraculous events occurred for you to be here. You are a miracle. May you acknowledge the intricate design that makes up your body - your cells, your neurons, your muscles. May you admire the connection your body has to your mind, your thoughts, and the ability you have to observe life around you with your sense of sight, touch, smell, taste, hearing, interpretation of communication, ability to connect, to love, to experience joy and laughter and happiness.

In this moment, observe yourself. Take in your hands, your body, your thoughts, the breath in your lungs. Feel the life within you. Take a deep breath and let it out slowly. Understand that life is a powerful, precious and miraculous thing you are experiencing. Remember that you get to live; you get to feel; you get to learn; you get to love. Today is an opportunity to live your life as best as you can. Even if you are having challenges, you can feel like you gave it your all by being your best. Even if you don't feel energized, you can learn to rest. Even if you don't enjoy what or who is in your life, you can learn to adopt changes in you and around you. Even if you don't see the magic or beauty in life, the fact remains that YOU are magic and you are beauty with that magnificent beating heart that is within you, with that breath in your lungs, with that ability to use your senses to witness the environment around you.

You are life. Therefore, go live fully and recharge yourself often.

Purpose

This exercise is a reminder to you that you are life! You are a miracle, and you can find joy because that is one of your natural states.
Be well. Live life.

Find more at **www.HappinessRecharge.com**.

www.ingramcontent.com/pod-product-compliance
Lightning Source LLC
Chambersburg PA
CBHW020541290526
45786CB00002B/983